Black Eyed Peas

by C.F. Earl

Superstars of Hip-Hop

Alicia Keys

Beyoncé

Black Eyed Peas

Ciara

Dr. Dre

Drake

Eminem

50 Cent

Flo Rida

Hip Hop:
A Short History

Jay-Z

Kanye West

Lil Wayne

LL Cool J

Ludacris

Mary J. Blige

Notorious B.I.G.

Rihanna

Sean "Diddy" Combs

Snoop Dogg

T.I.

T-Pain

Timbaland

Tupac

Usher

Black Eyed Peas

by C.F. Earl

Mason Crest

Black Eyed Peas

Mason Crest
370 Reed Road
Broomall, Pennsylvania 19008
www.masoncrest.com

Printed and bound in the United States of America.

First printing
9 8 7 6 5 4 3 2 1

Library of Congress Cataloging-in-Publication Data

Earl, C. F.
  Black Eyed Peas / by C.F. Earl.
     p. cm. − (Superstars of hip hop)
  Includes index.
  ISBN 978-1-4222-2511-0 (hardcover) − ISBN 978-1-4222-2508-0 (series hardcover) − ISBN 978-1-4222-2537-0 (softcover) − ISBN 978-1-4222-9213-6 (ebook)
 1. Black Eyed Peas (Musical group)−Juvenile literature. 2. Rap musicians−United States−Biography−Juvenile literature. I. Title.
  ML3930.B577E37 2012
  782.421649092'2−dc22
  [B]
                                    2011005426

Produced by Harding House Publishing Services, Inc.
www.hardinghousepages.com
Interior Design by MK Bassett-Harvey.
Cover design by Torque Advertising & Design.

Contents

Hip-Hop lingo

Breaking—also called b-boying or break dancing—is a style of hip-hop dancing. It involves spinning, headstands, and flips.

Rap is a kind of music where rhymes are chanted, often with music in the background. When people rap, they make up these rhymes, sometimes off the top of their heads.

DJ is short for disc jockey. A DJ plays music on the radio or at a party and announces the songs.

A **contract** is a written agreement between two people. Once you've signed a contract, it's against the law to break it. When a musician signs a contract with a music company, the musician promises to give all her music to that company for them to make as CDs and then sell—and the music company promises to pay the musician a certain amount of money. Usually, a contract is for a certain period of time.

A **label** is a company that produces music and sells CDs.

An **album** is a group of songs collected together on a CD.

A **single** is a song that is sold by itself.

Chapter 1

Beginnings

Today, the Black Eyed Peas are known around the world. Their music has been heard by millions of people. But the four Black Eyed Peas weren't always superstars. Their songs weren't always played on the radio, in clubs, or at parties.

Fergie, will.i.am, Taboo, and apl.de.ap were once just four hip-hop fans. They all loved music. They loved it so much they wanted to make their own. But it took a while for the Black Eyed Peas to find each other. It took a while for them to become the group that fans everywhere love today.

The Black Eyed Peas got their start when two high school friends got together.

William in Los Angeles

will.i.am's real name is William James Adams Jr. He was born on March 15, 1975.

William was an only child. He grew up in the projects of East Los Angeles. His mother raised him. William doesn't remember his father.

When apl.de.ap first came to the United States, he spoke no English. That didn't stop him from becoming friends with will.i.am, and this friendship and shared love of music and performing sowed the seeds for the Black Eyed Peas.

William was different from other kids in his neighborhood. He wore different clothes. He was quieter.

William's neighborhood had people of many different backgrounds. William went to an all-black church with his mom. He rode the school bus with mostly white kids. Lots of Mexican families lived in his neighborhood. William got along with everyone. It didn't matter where they were from or what they looked like.

William liked to hang out with all the kids at his school. He liked to move from one group to another. He talked to the black kids for a while. Then he talked to a group of Asian kids. He spent some time with white friends. Then he hung out with his Latino friends.

"If I didn't go to that school, Black Eyed Peas wouldn't be what it is," will.i.am said later. "I don't think we would be able to relate to every country on the planet."

William Meets Allan

Because he grew up in the kind of place he did, William learned how to get along with different kinds of people. He became best friends with Allan Pineda Lindo, Jr. Today, Allan is known as apl.de.ap.

Allan came from the Philippines. When William met him, Allan didn't know how to speak English. But the differences between them didn't keep them from becoming good friends.

Allan Pineda Lindo, Jr. was born on November 28, 1974, in the Philippines. Allan's father was a U.S. serviceman serving in the Philippines. Soon after Allan was born, his father left the family. Allan's mother raised him alone.

When Allan was young, he learned he had something wrong with his eyes. He had trouble controlling the movement of his eyes. He also had trouble seeing clearly.

An American group called the Pearl S. Buck Foundation helped Allan. The group connected Americans and children in Asia. Each American could give a little money every month to help a child live a better life. A man named Joe Ben Hudgens was the one who helped Allan.

When Joe learned about Allan's eye problems, he brought Allan to the United States. Allan was finally able to get some help with his condition. But when he saw more of the United States, he asked Joe if he could stay. Three years later, Allan's mother agreed to let Joe adopt him. It was a hard choice, but she decided Allan needed help from American doctors.

At fourteen years old, Allan moved from the Philippines to Los Angeles. In his new school, he became friends with William. The boys had a lot in common, even though they didn't speak the same language at first. They both loved music. They both loved to dance, too.

Tribal Nation and Atban Klann

William and Allan both loved **breaking**, a type of dancing also known as b-boying or break dancing. Through breaking, Allan learned more and more about hip-hop. It also helped William and Allan become better friends.

Soon, they started their own dance group. They called the group Tribal Nation. Tribal Nation started dancing at lots of parties and clubs in L.A.

In 1991, William and Allan decided they wanted to focus more on making music than on dancing. They decided to quit Tribal Nation. In its place, they started a **rap** group named Atban Klann. Atban stood for "A Tribe Beyond A Nation."

William began using the name Will-1X. Allan started going by apl.de.ap. They started talking to other people about joining Atban Klann. Rapper Mookie Mook and singer Dante Santiago joined the group. DJ Motiv8 became the group's **DJ**. Even with new members, Will-1X and apl.de.ap were the center of Atban Klann.

Ruthless Records

In 1992, Atban Klann signed a **contract** with Ruthless Records. Ruthless was owned and run by rapper Eazy-E. The **label** was known for its gangsta rap style. That music was very different from Atban Klann's happy messages.

Eazy-E didn't mind that Atban Klann was different, though. He included the group in one of his songs. Other people at Ruthless weren't as happy to have Atban Klann. They wondered what Eazy saw in the group.

Atban Klann recorded its first **album** in 1992. It was called *Grass Roots*. The album was never released, though. Instead, it was put aside for later. The album was just too different for Ruthless, no matter what Eazy thought. Though *Grass Roots* was supposed to come out at the end of 1992, it never did.

When Eazy-E died in 1995, Ruthless dropped Atban Klann. The group had put out one **single**, but they had never released an album. Atban Klann decided it was time to split up.

William and Allan weren't going to give up on their dreams. They were still very good friends. Soon, they were ready to start a new group. They wanted to keep trying to make it in the world of music. And it wouldn't be long before William and Allan found the right group to do just that.

Hip-Hop lingo

Lyrics are the words in a song.

Critics are people who judge artistic works and say what is good and what is bad about them.

A **soundtrack** is a collection of all the songs on a movie.

If you **produce** an album or a song, you're in charge of making the decisions about how it's performed, put together, and recorded.

The **singles chart** is a list of the best-selling songs for a week.

Chapter 2

Forming the Black Eyed Peas

William and Allan were on their own again. They were going to keep making music, though.

Their new group was first called the Black Eyed Pods. Soon, the name was changed and they became the Black Eyed Peas. William changed his rap name from Will-1X to will.i.am. The Black Eyed Peas were on their way!

But before they hit it big, the group needed more than just will.i.am and apl.de.ap. They found a third rapper to join the group. His name was Taboo.

Taboo Joins the Group

Taboo was born Jaime Luis Gómez. Jaime was born on July 14, 1975 in East Los Angeles. Jaime's family was Mexican, although his grandmother was Shoshone, a member of a Native American group that lives in the American West. He grew up speaking Spanish. He didn't know much about his Native American background.

From the beginning, the Black Eyed Peas were different from most of the other hip-hop artists. And it was a difference they were proud of. According to Taboo, they wanted the average listener—not just someone clued into the hip-hop scene—to be able to understand their lyrics.

Jaime grew up in a Latino neighborhood. He loved music and dancing. Jaime loved hip-hop more than any other type of music. He liked to wear chains and baggy clothes, just like his favorite rappers. Some kids made fun of Jaime for being a Mexican kid who wore gold chains and listened to rap. But he didn't care.

In 1995, Jaime met will.i.am and apl.de.ap at a club. Jaime was mostly a dancer at that time. But soon, he became the third member of the Black Eyed Peas. He finally had a place to fit in. In the Peas, Jaime got to rap. He could be involved with hip-hop without people thinking he didn't belong.

With Taboo in the group, the Black Eyed Peas were ready to move on. Singer Kim Hill also started to perform with the group.

The Black Eyed Peas began playing shows with a live band. Most rappers perform with a DJ who plays the music. But the Black Eyed Peas wanted to do things differently. They had a full group of musicians play with them. They didn't do what other artists were doing.

The group's music was also different. They didn't sound like the popular gangsta rap of the early 1990s. They didn't rap about guns and violence. They made music about having a good time and staying happy. They didn't wear the same kind of clothes as other rappers, either.

Their shows, style, and **lyrics** all showed that the Black Eyed Peas weren't like other rap groups.

Behind the Front

The Black Eyed Peas kept playing shows. They tried to get their music out to more people. Soon, Interscope Records was ready to sign a contract with the group. The Black Eyed Peas joined the label. They started work on their first album.

The Black Eyed Peas' first album was called *Behind the Front*. It was released on June 30, 1998.

Many of the songs on *Behind the Front* were recorded for *Grass Roots* in 1992. Since that album wasn't going to be released, the Black Eyed Peas used some of the same songs on *Behind the Front*.

When the album came out, many **critics** thought it was very good. They liked that the album focused on such happy messages. They also thought the live band gave the group a different kind of sound.

Though critics liked the album, it didn't sell very well. The Black Eyed Peas gained a lot of new fans with the album, but it wasn't a big success.

The album had three singles. The first was called "Fallin' Up." The song was about how the Peas were different from other hip-hop artists. In the song, the group rapped about how they didn't want to do what was popular just to have people buy their music. The song wasn't a hit, but it gave new listeners an idea of who the Black Eyed Peas were.

The second single was called "Joints and Jam." It featured Kim Hill. In 1998, "Joints and Jam" was included on the **soundtrack** to the movie *Bulworth*. Thanks to the success of the soundtrack, the song did better than "Fallin' Up."

"Karma" was the third single from *Behind the Front*. This song didn't do as well as the Black Eyed Peas had hoped it would, either.

Bridging the Gap

On September 26, 2000, the Black Eyed Peas released their second album. It was called *Bridging the Gap*.

will.i.am and apl.de.ap helped **produce** the album. DJ Premier, Wonder, and Rhett Lawrence helped them. Kim Hill sang on a few songs for *Bridging the Gap*. Around this time, though, she stopped working with the Black Eyed Peas. *Bridging the Gap* also featured De La Soul, Mos Def, and Macy Gray.

Bridging the Gap had three singles. The first was called "BEP Empire." It made it to the Hot Rap **singles chart**. It wasn't a big hit for the group, though.

The second single was called "Weekends." This song did better than "BEP Empire." The third single was called "Request + Line." The song featured Macy Gray. It was the most successful single from *Bridging the Gap*.

Like many groups, the Black Eyed Peas had growing pains, which included a variety of lineups. In time, the Peas settled on the members that would bring the group fame—and mega sales.

Like *Behind the Front, Bridging the Gap* was popular with critics. The fans of the Black Eyed Peas loved it too. But the group still wasn't as big as they would be later. It would take some hard work—and adding one more member to the group—to get them there.

Hard Times

After *Bridging the Gap* came out, the Black Eyed Peas took a break. Around that time, apl.de.ap got a letter from his family in the Philippines. His brother had committed suicide. Then apl.de.ap and his girlfriend split up.

One of the group's earliest hits was "Where Is the Love?" They wrote the song after the September 11, 2001, terrorist attacks on the United States. The song was their way of dealing with the aftermath of the horrific events of that day.

apl.de.ap was very sad. He started using drugs to try to get away from his problems. Soon, he was addicted to crystal meth.

apl.de.ap's manager saw that the rapper had a problem. He knew apl.de.ap needed someone to help him. One day, apl.de.ap thought he was going shopping with his manager. Instead, the two drove to a rehab clinic—a place where apl.de.ap could get help becoming free from his addiction.

At first, apl.de.ap was angry about being tricked. But he also knew he needed help. He knew he needed to make a change in his life. After two visits to the clinic, apl.de.ap quit using drugs. And he stayed clean!

At the same time, Taboo was having trouble with alcohol. The Black Eyed Peas were struggling. They didn't like where they were headed.

Just before the group started their third album, terrorists attacked the United States on September 11, 2001. The attacks made will.i.am, apl.de.ap, and Taboo realize they wouldn't live forever. It made the group understand they needed to change their lives.

After the attacks of September 11th, will.i.am wanted to make music that would help people through the hard times. So they made a song called "Where Is the Love?"

The Black Eyed Peas knew their next album would have to be special. The group was ready to make it happen. But first, they needed one more member in the group.

Hip-Hop lingo

Producers are the people in charge of putting together songs. A producer makes the big decisions about the music.

Studios are places where musicians go to record their music and turn it into CDs.

Chapter 3

Finding Fergie

Fergie's real name is Stacy Ferguson. She was born in Hacienda Heights, California, near Los Angeles.

Stacy's parents both taught in Catholic schools. Her dad was a vice principal and geography teacher. Her mother taught kids with disabilities.

Stacy always loved to perform. As a kid, she danced and sang whenever she could. She wanted to be a singer more than anything else.

When she was eight years old, Stacy started working as a voice actor. She worked on commercials and TV shows. She voiced Sally for *The Charlie Brown and Snoopy Show* in 1985. She also acted in a few television shows.

Stacy's biggest acting job was a show called *Kids Incorporated*. She started working on the show in 1984. Her part involved singing and acting. By 1989, Stacy was ready to move on from *Kids Incorporated*. It had been a great time for Stacy, but she still wanted to be a singer.

A few years after Stacy left *Kids Incorporated*, she started a singing group with two other girls from the show. The group was called Wild Orchid.

Wild Orchid

Stacy's dream had always been to become a singer. She'd always wanted to perform in front of people. Now, she finally had her chance. But things didn't turn out the way she hoped.

Wild Orchid put out two albums. Neither did very well, though. The group had some fans. The girls worked hard. But the group never became what Stacy wanted it to be.

Stacy thought about leaving the group. She thought she might start her own music career. But she didn't know how to tell the other girls in the group. She didn't want to hurt their feelings. So instead, she stayed. She didn't feel good about being in the group anymore, though.

Stacy felt worse and worse about Wild Orchid. She was also feeling worse and worse about herself. She didn't want to stay in the group. But she didn't feel she could leave. Stacy turned to drugs to get away from her problems.

At first, she thought she was just having fun. But soon, she realized she wasn't just partying. She was addicted. Stacy needed help.

A friend gave her the help she needed. Stacy stopped using drugs. Now she knew it was time to leave Wild Orchid. Then she also moved in with her parents. She told her friends and family what had been happening in her life.

Stacy had beaten her drug addiction. But she was still looking for a way to make her dream of being a singer come true.

Joining the Black Eyed Peas

The money Stacy had made as a child actor was gone. She had used it all to pay the debts she owed people because of her drug problem. Without any money, all Stacy had was her dream of being a singer.

Though Wild Orchard cut a couple of albums, neither was particularly memorable. Fergie wanted to leave the group, but she didn't want to hurt the other members. So she stayed, a decision that played a role in Fergie's drug abuse.

Over the years, the Black Eyed Peas' skills have brought them to many red-carpet events. Whether it's the Soul Train Music Awards or a charity event, the Peas are often asked to participate.

She started looking for someone she could work with to make music. She looked for songwriters and **producers**. She looked for **studios**. At the same time, the Black Eyed Peas were looking for a new sound.

will.i.am was looking for a female singer for a song called "Shut Up." Dante Santiago told will.i.am about a singer who was calling herself Fergie. Dante had been in Atban Klann with will.i.am and apl.de.ap. will.i.am trusted him.

Years earlier, the Black Eyed Peas had met Fergie when she was still with Wild Orchid. Now, will.i.am had a chance to work with Fergie in the studio. He knew something special was happening. He told Fergie she'd be great for the song.

She started spending more time with the Peas. She worked with the group very well. They wanted to make her part of the Black Eyed Peas for good. Soon, Fergie became the fourth member of the group. Her dream had come true!

The Black Eyed Peas family was complete. With Fergie on board, there was nothing stopping the group. They were ready to take on the world.

Hip-Hop lingo

Each year, the National Academy of Recording Arts and Sciences gives out the Grammy Awards (short for Gramophone Awards)—or **Grammys**—to people who have done something really big in the music industry. When something has been **nominated**, it has been picked as one of the things that might win an award.

Solo means by yourself. A solo artist sings by herself instead of with a group.

Chapter 4

The Peas Become Stars

At the end of 2001, the Black Eyed Peas started work on their third album. It was called *Elephunk*.

The group started working on *Elephunk* before they met Fergie. They met her during recording. She joined the Black Eyed Peas while they were making the album.

The first single from *Elephunk* was called "Where Is the Love?" The song was co-written by Justin Timberlake. He also sings the chorus of the song. "Where Is the Love?" was a huge hit for the Black Eyed Peas. The song made it to number eight on the Hot 100 singles chart. It was their most successful song so far. It was also their first top-ten single.

"Shut Up" was their next single. This was the first song they had worked on with Fergie. "Shut Up" was a huge hit in Australia and Europe. It hit number one in many countries.

The third single was called "Hey Mama." Like "Shut Up," this song was a huge hit in Europe.

"The Apl Song," written by apl.de.ap, is influenced by his Filipino heritage. The chorus is in Tagalog, his native language. apl.de.ap is very proud of his heritage and homeland.

Elephunk's fourth single was called "Let's Get It Started." The song was another big hit. "Let's Get It Started" made it to twenty-one on the Hot 100 singles chart.

Elephunk was released on June 24, 2003. Thanks to its singles, the album made it to number fourteen on the album charts. Today, it has sold more than three million copies in the United States. *Elephunk* has sold more than eight million copies around the world.

At the 2004 **Grammys**, the Black Eyed Peas performed "Where Is the Love?" The song was **nominated** for two Grammy awards. The next year, the Peas won a Grammy for Best Rap Performance by a Duo or Group for "Let's Get It Started."

The Black Eyed Peas wasn't an unknown rap group anymore. Now, they were worldwide pop stars. "Where Is the Love?" and "Let's Get It Started" were played everywhere. The Black Eyed Peas had reached new levels with *Elephunk*.

Monkey Business

After *Elephunk*, the Black Eyed Peas started work on their next album. It was called *Monkey Business*. It went on sale on May 27, 2005.

The first single from *Monkey Business* was called "Don't Phunk with My Heart." The song made it to number three on the Hot 100 singles chart. It was the second Black Eyed Peas song to reach the top ten.

The album's second single, "Don't Lie," was released a few months later. The song made it to number fourteen on the singles chart. Another song on the album, "My Humps," started getting radio play before "Don't Lie" was released as a single. "My Humps" was released as a single in September, after being played all summer. The song reached number three on the singles chart.

"Pump It" was the fourth single from *Monkey Business*. It had hit the singles chart in the summer of 2005. When it was officially released as a single, early in 2006, the song hit the charts again.

Monkey Business was a huge success for the Black Eyed Peas. *Elephunk* put them in the spotlight. *Monkey Business* proved they were there to stay. With help from its singles, *Monkey Business* sold very well. In the week it came out, it sold around 295,000 copies. Today, the album has sold millions of copies around the world.

At the 2006 Grammys, the Black Eyed Peas won Best Rap Performance by a Duo or Group for "Don't Phunk with My Heart." They were also nominated for four Grammys for songs from *Monkey Business*. In 2007, they won Best Pop Performance by a Duo or Group with Vocal Grammy award for "My Humps."

Monkey Business proved the Black Eyed Peas could keep making huge hit songs after *Elephunk*. The album also kept them popular all over the world. With *Monkey Business*, the Black Eyed Peas became one of the biggest groups in the world of music.

Going Solo

After the success of *Monkey Business*, the Black Eyed Peas started to work on many different projects.

Fergie released her first **solo** album in September of 2006. The album was called *The Dutchess*. The album had three number-one singles. "London Bridge," "Glamorous," and "Big Girls Don't Cry" all made it to the top spot on the Hot 100 singles chart. "Fergalicious" and "Clumsy" were also huge hit singles from the album. *The Dutchess* has sold more than three million albums in the United States alone.

will.i.am also put out a solo album after *Monkey Business*. He'd released two solo albums earlier. Those albums weren't as well known as his work after *Elephunk*, though. In 2001, he'd put out *Lost Change.* In 2003, he'd released *Must B 21*. Neither album was very successful.

In 2007, though, he put out *Songs About Girls*. will.i.am said he thought of *Songs About Girls* as his first solo album. He said his other two albums were more based around music he made as a producer, rather than as an artist.

Songs About Girls didn't sell as well as the Black Eyed Peas albums or Fergie's album. It sold around 20,000 copies its first week out. It seemed will.i.am wasn't as successful on his own as he was with the Black Eyed Peas. But he didn't mind. He was also working on producing music for other artists. He was working on new projects, too.

New Things for the Black Eyed Peas

Solo albums and new music projects weren't the only thing the Black Eyed Peas were doing after *Monkey Business*. They were also acting in movies and on TV.

Fergie had been an actor when she was younger. So it wasn't hard for her to move from music back to acting. In 2005, Fergie had a role in *Poseidon*. In 2007, she played Tammy in *Grindhouse*. Two years later, she played Saraghina in the musical movie *Nine*.

Fergie also did some voice acting for animated movies. Her voice can be heard in *Madagascar 2* and *Marmaduke*. Voice acting was something Fergie knew a lot about. After all, she'd done voice acting for Charlie Brown cartoons when she was younger.

will.i.am also started acting. In 2005, he was in an episode of the TV show *Joan of Arcadia*. Two years later, he was in an episode of *Cane*. He also had a role in *X-Men Origins: Wolverine* in 2009. Like Fergie, will.i.am lent his voice to *Madagascar 2.*

Away from the Black Eyed Peas, will.i.am is keeping very busy. He has a clothing line, a record label, produces work for other performers, and writes and performs his own work.

will.i.am was also getting involved in politics. During the 2008 presidential election, will.i.am made a song in support of Barack Obama. The song was called "Yes We Can." will.i.am got the lyrics from a speech Obama gave during his campaign.

When Barack Obama was elected president, will.i.am made a song called "It's a New Day." He wrote the song to celebrate the election of the first black President of the United States.

The Black Eyed Peas had become superstars all over the world. Their songs were being heard everywhere. *Elephunk* and *Monkey Business* had taken the group to new places. The Black Eyed Peas were as famous as musical groups get. The group wasn't going to slow down, either.

Hip-Hop lingo

Tracks are parts–usually songs–of an album.

Pop is short for "popular." Pop music is usually light and happy, with a good beat.

Techno is a kind of dance music with an electronic sound and heavy beat.

Chapter 5

Another Beginning

The Black Eyed Peas had become stars around the world. They'd taken some time to make their own music. Some fans thought the group would split up. They thought Fergie might just keep making her own albums. They thought will.i.am might start producing music full-time or put out more albums of his own.

Instead, the Black Eyed Peas went to work on their next album. The album was called *The E.N.D.* That was short for "The Energy Never Dies." It was released on June 3, 2009.

With *The E.N.D.*, the Black Eyed Peas changed their sound. They moved away from their hip-hop sound. *The E.N.D.* had a much more **techno** sound than *Elephunk* or *Monkey Business*. will.i.am said the new album's sound was based on music he'd heard in Australian clubs.

The Black Eyed Peas put out five singles from *The E.N.D.* The first was "Boom Boom Pow." It was released two months before the album came out.

"Boom Boom Pow" was downloaded almost half a million times its first week out. The song shot to number one on the Hot 100 singles chart. Then it stayed there for twelve weeks.

The second single from *The E.N.D.* was called "I Gotta Feeling." David Guetta, a DJ from France, produced the song. When "I Gotta Feeling" first came out, it was the number-two single in the United States. "Boom Boom Pow" was still in the top spot. The Black Eyed Peas were one of very few artists to ever have both the number-one and number-two songs on the chart.

Soon, "I Gotta Feeling" reached number one. "I Gotta Feeling" stayed at number one for fourteen weeks. That meant the Black Eyed Peas had the number-one song in the country for twenty-six weeks straight. That's half a year!

The third single, "Meet Me Halfway," reached number seven on the charts. The fourth single, "Rock That Body," made it to number nine.

The last single from *The E.N.D.* was called "Imma Be." The song was another huge hit for the group. "Imma Be" reached number one on the singles chart in early 2010. It was the third number-one song from *The E.N.D.*

The E.N.D. was a huge success all over the world. The album sold more than 300,000 copies in its first week. It was also the number-one album in the United States that week. Today, the album has sold more than 11 million copies around the globe.

At the 2010 Grammy Awards, the Black Eyed Peas were nominated for six awards. *The E.N.D.* was nominated for Album of the Year. The group won Best **Pop** Performance by a Duo or Group with Vocals for "I Gotta Feeling." They also won Best Pop Vocal Album for *The E.N.D.*

The Beginning

In the summer of 2010, the Black Eyed Peas told an interviewer they were working on their next album. will.i.am said the new album would be a sequel to *The E.N.D.* He said the album would be a new start for the group.

In October, the Black Eyed Peas announced the name of their new album. It was called *The Beginning.* The album was released the next month, on November 26, 2010.

will.i.am produced many of the **tracks** on *The Beginning*. For some, he had help from other producers. David Guetta, who produced "I Gotta Feeling," helped out with one song. That song was called "The Best One Yet (The Boy)." DJ Ammo also helped produce songs on the album. He produced the song "Do It Like This," and helped on others. DJ Ammo also helped produce the album's first single.

The Beginning's first single was called "The Time (Dirty Bit)." The song's chorus is pulled from another song called "(I've Had) The Time of My Life." It was originally on the soundtrack to the 1987 movie *Dirty Dancing*.

"The Time (Dirty Bit)" was released in early November of 2010. By early December, the song was in the top ten. "The Time" was the Peas' ninth song to make it so far up the charts. The song was also a number-one hit in many countries.

The Beginning was the number-six album in the United States its first week out. The album sold 119,000 copies in the United States that week. *The E.N.D.* had sold more in its first week, but *The Beginning* came out the same week as many other big albums.

Though *The Beginning* started slow, the Black Eyed Peas didn't slow down. In February 2011, they performed at the half-time show of the Super Bowl. Only the biggest musical acts are chosen for the Super Bowl. The Black Eyed Peas had become one of the most famous groups in the world.

Looking to the Future

The Black Eyed Peas have gone from small rap group to **pop** stars known in countries around the world. The group's one-of-a-kind sound and style have helped them connect to fans everywhere.

Taboo has pursued a solo career as well, including an album in Spanish. He's also started an acting career and a nonprofit school of the arts. Taboo knows it's important to give back to the community.

Their music has touched the lives of millions of people. They have fans all over the globe. Their songs are played in clubs and at parties, in bedrooms and in stadiums, on the radio and TV.

Like their music, the group's struggles carry a message. The fact that they all come from such different backgrounds is also a message. Music can help anyone get through tough times, no matter his or her background. Music can help bring people together. No matter where we are from or what we look like, we can all enjoy music!

Few groups have done what the Peas have done in music. Few artists are as famous in as many countries as the Black Eyed Peas are today.

In July 2011, the Peas announced that they'd be taking a break from making music and performing together. The group said that they hadn't broken up. The Black Eyed Peas needed some time off from being one of the biggest acts in the world.

No one can be sure what the Black Eyed Peas will do after their break. Fans wonder if they'll change their sound, like they did with *The E.N.D.* The members of the group might choose to put out more solo albums. Maybe they'll choose to do more acting on TV and in movies.

No matter what the Black Eyed Peas do next, millions of fans around the world will be waiting.

Late 1960s–1970s
Break dancing develops.

Nov. 28, 1974
Allen Pineda, apl.de.ap, is born.

July 14, 1975
Jaime Gomez, Taboo, is born.

Mar. 15, 1975
William Adams, will.i.am, is born.

Mar. 27, 1975
Stacy Ferguson, Fergie, is born.

1977 Modern break dancing develops.

1998 The group's first album is released.

2000 *Bridging the Gap*, the group's second album, is released.

2001 will.i.am's first solo album is released.

2003 "Where Is the Love" becomes the group's first top-10 hit.

2003 *Elephunk* is released, the first album to feature Fergie.

2004 The Black Eyed Peas perform in a series of concerts to encourage young people to vote.

2004 The Black Eyed Peas win their first Grammy Award.

2005 *Monkey Business* is released.

2005 The group establishes the Black Eyed Peas' Peapod Foundation.

2005 The group performs at Live 8.

2006   Fergie's first solo album, *The Duchess*, is released.

2006   Fergie performs in the film *Poseidon*.

2007   Fergie appears in the film *Grindhouse*.

July 7, 2007

Black Eyed Peas perform at the London venue of the Live Earth concert series.

June 2009

The Black Eyed Peas release their fifth studio album, *The E.N.D.*

2009-2010

The E.ND. World Tour, which consists of 108 shows, hits five continents.

The Black Eyed Peas release their fifth studio album, *The Beginning*.

2011   The Black Eyed Peas announce they are taking a break from making music and touring.

Discography

Albums

1998	Behind the Front
2000	Bridging the Gap
2003	Elephunk
2005	Monkey Business
2006	Renegotiations: The Remixes
2009	The E.N.D. (Energy Never Dies)
2010	The Beginning

DVDs

2004	Behind the Bridge to Elephunk
2006	Live from Sydney to Vegas
2007	Black Eyed Peas
2010	The E.N.D. World Tour

Books

Baker, Soren. *The History of Rap and Hip Hop*. San Diego, Calif.: Lucent, 2006.

Comissiong, Solomon W. F. *How Jamal Discovered Hip-Hop Culture*. New York: Xlibris, 2008.

Cornish, Melanie. *The History of Hip Hop*. New York: Crabtree, 2009.

Czekaj, Jef. *Hip and Hop, Don't Stop!* New York: Hyperion, 2010.

Haskins, Jim. *One Nation Under a Groove: Rap Music and Its Roots*. New York: Jump at the Sun, 2000.

Hatch, Thomas. *A History of Hip-Hop: The Roots of Rap*. Portsmouth, N.H.: Red Bricklearning, 2005.

Websites

Black Eyed Peas
music.aol.com/artist/black-eyed-peas

Black Eyed Peas
www.starpulse.com/Music/Black_Eyed_Peas

Black Eyed Peas Official Website
www.blackeyedpeas.com

Fergie
fergie.blackeyedpeas.com

will.i.am
will-i-am.blackeyedpeas.com

Index

Picture Credits

istockphotos: p. 18
PR Photos: p. 23
      Alan, Scott: p. 14
      Harris, Glenn: pp. 8, 20
      Hatcher, Chris: pp. 1, 24, 26, 28, 32, 38
      Lau, Tina: p. 12
      Mayer, Janet: p. 6
      Moore, Anthony: p. 17
      Thompson, Terry: p. 34

To the best knowledge of the publisher, all other images are in the public domain. If any image has been inadvertently uncredited, please notify Harding House Publishing Services, Vestal, New York 13850, so that rectification can be made for future printings.

About the Author

C.F. Earl is a writer living and working in Binghamton, New York. Earl writes mostly on social and historical topics, including health, the military, and finances. An avid student of the world around him, and particularly fascinated with almost any current issue, C.F. Earl hopes to continue to write for books, websites, and other publications for as long as he is able.